Self EMS

**GARY
HAYWOOD**

SELF EMS

Publisher: GH WOOD LLC
Printed in U.S.A.
First Printing, 2025

Your *sacrifice*, no matter how small, is everything to **Him**.

"Because your sacrifice is important to me." – **JC**

"I must be made of sterner stuff."

TABLE OF CONTENTS

The Goal

Self-Empowerment

Self-Motivation

Self-Sustainability

Why It Works

Rewards of Success

The goal is simple.

Achieve perpetual success by mastering these 3 pillars.

Self-Empowerment

Self-Motivation

Self-Sustainability

The foundational "Truths of Success".

Self-Empowerment

Power and Knowledge

Knowledge is nothing without application: Knowledge on its own is inert. It's the action that transforms understanding into results.

Power is the application of knowledge: Knowledge alone doesn't give you control over your life. It's when you apply what you know to shape your actions, decisions, and outcomes that you gain power.

Self-Empowerment is the application of power in one's own life: It's not just about having knowledge or power in abstract terms, but about consciously applying that power to direct your life, making choices that reflect your values, goals, and strengths.

Use critical thinking and research as tools to empower yourself: These tools help you discern useful knowledge from useless distraction. They(tools) sharpen your mind and give you the ability to question, analyze, and decide what serves you.

Commit to lifelong learning to empower yourself: Growth never stops. The more you learn, the more adaptable and resilient you become. Lifelong learning ensures that you stay relevant, flexible, and ready for the unknown. Every new thing you learn is a new tool for your personal empowerment.

Never relent and always continue to challenge yourself: Growth doesn't happen without persistence. Resilience is key to success, and that means never giving up. Each challenge is an opportunity to expand your capacity, and every setback/failure can become a learning experience that strengthens you.

Take charge of your own evolution because self-empowerment is not a passive state.

You learn (knowledge), then you apply that knowledge (power), and you empower yourself through consistent action and self-determination.

You question and research in order to make sure your knowledge is valid and applicable. Commit to growth so that you don't stagnate.

Challenges become the fuel for growth, and relentlessness ensures you keep advancing. This is the kind of mindset that doesn't just react to life—it shapes it.

Self-empowerment allows you to be the architect of your own reality.

Self-Motivation

The Drive Within

Your individuality is your signature—unique and irreplaceable: It's your essence—your personality, your experiences, and the perspective you offer. No one else can replicate that.

Life is often framed in terms of binary outcomes—either we succeed, or we fail.

When you rely on people or substances, you become vulnerable to circumstances outside your control. True motivation comes from within. When you take ownership of your drive, you have a consistent, internal source of energy.

One needs to channel the emotional energy from every failure, mistake, or hardship. Each carries emotional energy—that surge of frustration, sadness, or anger can either be wasted or used as fuel for growth. Channeling that energy properly is the key to resilience.

Doing the right thing fuels internal drive: There's something deeply fulfilling about knowing you're aligned with your core values. When you make decisions that resonate with your integrity, that internal moral compass provides an unshakable sense of purpose.

External success—money, status, recognition—can sometimes obscure what truly matters:

Internal Happiness and Peace

A high-quality life doesn't always have to mean chasing after societal benchmarks of success.

A philosophy of self-reliance, inner strength, and authenticity. The rewards of life come from understanding who you are by cultivating your inner motivation.

You don't need to rely on anyone else to define who you are or what you can achieve. Ensure success becomes inevitable.

Self-motivation is found within: your individuality, your drive, and your ability to rise from challenges.

Self-Sustainability

Making It Last

By practicing mindfulness, you cultivate awareness of the present moment, which helps you detach from emotional turbulence. This allows you to observe your thoughts and emotions without being overwhelmed by them, maintaining balance no matter what is happening around us.

Challenging your mind: improves cognitive flexibility and increases confidence. The process of learning and adapting helps you build mental endurance as well.

The more you practice "emotional regulation", the less likely external situations or people can destabilize you. Autonomy. Knowing you have the power to navigate challenges on your own, without excessive reliance on others, nurtures your inner strength and self-worth.

Stress is inevitable, but the way you approach it defines you. Building self-esteem and confidence is about acknowledging your achievements and failures, big or small, and recognizing your ability to grow through them.

It's not about avoiding tough situations; it's about developing the strength to face and adapt to them without losing your sense of self.

Cultivating gratitude shifts our focus from what's lacking to what's present and good. Even on tough days, practicing gratitude helps you reconnect with the positives in life, which boosts mental clarity and helps maintain a sense of purpose.

Self-sustainability helps you develop mental skills that allow you to: maintain clarity, focus, and well-being, regardless of external stressors.

Why It Works

Empowerment (Learning & Questioning)

Empowerment starts with gaining knowledge and becoming informed. Learning continuously and questioning the status quo helps you make informed decisions and shape your path with confidence.

Motivation (Purpose & Consistency)

Motivation is the driving force that helps you take action. When you know why you're doing something, you gain a sense of purpose. But it's not just about the initial spark—it's about staying consistent and focused. Purpose keeps you grounded, while consistency ensures that you keep pushing forward, even when obstacles arise.

Sustainability (Resilience & Self-Awareness)

Growth isn't linear, and challenges are inevitable. Building resilience helps you not only cope but also learn from difficulties. Self-awareness ensures that you understand your strengths, weaknesses, and emotional triggers, giving you the insight needed to keep evolving throughout a lifetime.

The Rewards of Success

Perpetual Success is a concept that goes beyond the traditional view of success as just achieving a goal or hitting a milestone. It's about creating a sustained state of growth, fulfillment, and well-being that continuously compounds over time.

This combination creates a holistic approach to self-growth: by learning and questioning, you empower yourself; by having purpose and staying consistent, you stay motivated; and by being resilient and self-aware, you sustain long-term growth.

All of these elements are interconnected. When you focus on one, you indirectly strengthen the others. This kind of mental sustainability doesn't just help you manage stress, but it also enhances your ability to enjoy life and find peace within, no matter what's happening externally.

As you continually improve in each of these areas (Self-Mastery), the cycle reinforces itself. The more empowered you feel, the more motivated you'll become. The more motivated you are, the more sustainable your efforts will be. And the more sustainable your efforts, the more empowered you'll feel — leading to continuous growth and achievement.

Gary Haywood is a first-time author whose debut work, *Self E.M.S.: Implementing Perpetual Success*, reflects his lifelong dedication to personal growth and resilience.

Born and raised in San Jose, California, Gary graduated from Yerba Buena High School before continuing his education at San José State University, San José City College, Evergreen Valley College, and later the University of Phoenix online. Each step in his academic journey added new perspectives that shaped his approach to perseverance, adaptability, and the pursuit of success.

Now at age 47, Gary resides in the suburbs of Boston, Massachusetts. His experiences across diverse communities and institutions have fueled his passion for empowering others to break cycles, embrace discipline, and cultivate sustainable success. *Self E.M.S.* is the culmination of that vision—a guide designed to inspire readers to take control of their lives and achieve lasting fulfillment.

www.ingramcontent.com/pod-product-compliance
Lightning Source LLC
Chambersburg PA
CBHW031242120626
46545CB00003B/1248